uman

The Essays

First published in Italy
in 2011 by
Skira Editore S.p.A.
Palazzo Casati Stampa
via Torino 61
20123 Milano
Italy
www.skira.net

Printed and bound in Italy.
First edition

ISBN: 978-88-572-0981-4

Distributed in USA, Canada, Central
& South America by Rizzoli International
Publications, Inc., 300 Park Avenue
South, New York, NY 10010, USA.
Distributed elsewhere in the world
by Thames and Hudson Ltd.,
181A High Holborn, London WC1V 7QX,
United Kingdom.

Christopher Dickey

monoi
paradise imagined

SKIRA

U

I want to thank my good friend Umberto
Angeloni for saving me from the winter.
On a gray October day in gray New York
he asked me to write about Paradise,
a place I have yet to visit, but that
so many other writers and painters
have explored in their books, on their
canvases, and in their dreams, that
I dared to think I might imagine
it through their fantasies and memories
(which were often the same).
I thought that, immersing myself
in their work, I might even experience
a few moments of the sublime in that
half-dreaming space between sleep
and waking, which is where I expect one
day to find my own stairway to Heaven.
So in the last months of 2010, as the days
in New York and in Paris, my other home,
grew shorter and darker and wetter
and colder, I read deep into the literature
of the South Seas, which is the closest
thing to Paradise that Europeans ever

discovered. I went to the Musée d'Orsay
to look at the paintings of those who
had made the journey across the oceans,
like Paul Gauguin, and those who had
made it only in their mind, like Henri
Rousseau, to see what colors and patterns
and tales hiding within the four corners
of their stretched *toiles* could take us
back to the portals of Eden, if not into its
luxuriant depths. I went to the recently
reconstructed and reopened Grand
Serre—the great hothouse—at the Jardin
des Plantes in the 13th *arrondissement*
of Paris to feel the steam and breathe
the promiscuity of dripping leaves and
succulent dirt. I closed my eyes
and smelled the loam and imagined the
faraway warmth of a land and a people.
What was missing, precisely, was the
color. Even Gauguin, with his bold strokes
of red and yellow, white and blue and
black, and his multi-hued browns—that
world of primary contrasts

he saw and shaped through that green eye you see in his best self-portrait— even *goddamn Gauguin* did not quite capture the cerulean glories of the Marquesas and the Society Islands of Polynesia. The most clichéd digital image on the Internet today is more stunning as a representation, but still does not do justice to the subject. Heaven, after all, cannot be as commonplace as a Ministry of Tourism Web site, and the beauty of these islands left great writers speechless. **At the beginning of the twentieth century, Somerset Maugham found a place at the end of a long dirt path in Tahiti that "had the beauty of the Garden of Eden," he said. "Ah, I wish I could make you see the enchantment of that spot, a corner hidden away from all the world, with the blue sky overhead and the rich,**

luxuriant trees. It was a feast of color. And it was fragrant and cool. Words cannot describe that paradise," wrote Maugham, who was never otherwise at a loss for words. **Generations of writers came and saw and were enraptured by the islands: Herman Melville and Robert Louis Stevenson, Jack London and Jacques Brel and hundreds if not thousands of others, decade after decade, then century after century.** They were fascinated by the uninhibited nudity they encountered but also by the simple elegance and comfort of **the *pareu*, which Stevenson liked to compare to a kilt, but so much lighter, so much cooler.** They claimed to be horrified, but just as often were mesmerized by the twirling designs of the tattoos on men and on women. Again and again they were

struck dumb by these places and these
peoples, who were called savages even
and especially when they showed more
decency than any of those adventurers
arriving on their shores from Europe.
It was on the shortest of December days
in Paris, which seemed still shorter
and darker than usual, with heavy flakes
of wet gray snow descending from the
gray sky to the gray sidewalks, that
what should have been an obvious truth
suddenly hit me like a revelation.
I was reading **Stevenson's *In the
South Seas***, watching him struggle
valiantly, as others had, to capture
the essence of the place.
**"Few men who come to the
islands leave them," he wrote,
"they grow grey where they
alighted; the palm shades and
the trade-wind fans them till
they die, perhaps cherishing
to the last the fancy of a visit**

home, which is rarely made, more rarely enjoyed, and yet more rarely repeated. No part of the world exerts the same attractive power upon the visitor, and the task before me is to communicate to fireside travelers some sense of its seduction."

You see what he is getting at here. One must be enticed by duty to leave such a paradise, and duty is not enough to keep you from being called back to the beach, to the palms, to the breezes and to the touch of the people there. No part of the European's world in the eighteenth or nineteenth or twentieth century was so profoundly redolent of both sex and innocence. "The first love, the first sunrise, the first South Sea island, are memories apart and touched virginity of sense," said Stevenson.

No promise of *houris* in the afterlife ever held more allure than the flesh and blood beauties of Tahiti. And the reaction of the righteous Westerners was, to call it what it was, fear. And that was what I understood as I looked up from the page in Paris at the snow coming down outside the window.

Those first pale visitors to the islands, for all their swords and muskets, cannons and shot, had been afraid of Paradise, of course, not because they did not understand what it was, but because they understood only too well. One might be, as Jack London wrote, "the inevitable white man, who, with Bible, bullet, or rum bottle, has confronted the amazed savage in his every stronghold," but somehow that wasn't enough to protect you from happiness. However it is that one finally arrives

at the celestial Heaven, it must be,
at first, as daunting a place to discover
yourself as the subterranean Hell;
either would have so little to do with
the quotidian lives we've known. **But
heaven on earth as it appeared
in the South Seas challenged
the essential worth of what
sailors, captains, scientists
and traders, not to mention
missionaries, believed were
their hard-won Christian
European virtues.** Such is the
innate fear of death's unknowns that
it takes a hellish present to make
us long for a blissful afterlife—but
if the present itself is sublime, what
promise would the hereafter hold?
And why would we make vows to priests
or gods to attain it?
You see the quandary of the Westerners,
and the threat to their notions of sin,
of redemption, of civilization.

As Rod Edmond wrote in his wonderful scholarly study, *Representing the South Pacific: Colonial Discourse from Cook to Gauguin*, the guilt-ridden **English missionaries who went to Tahiti and Bora Bora in the early nineteenth century might as well have been in Hell, so many of them were tempted to sin, as they saw it, and so many succumbed.** "In Britain it was women who fell," wrote Edmond, "in Tahiti it was missionaries." **Protectively, vindictively, missionaries insisted the men of the islands wear trousers and women cover their bodies in shapeless "Mother Hubbard" dresses.** Until, at last, the diseases brought by the Europeans so decimated the island populations that by the time Robert Louis Stevenson visited those far-flung atolls and

volcanic outcroppings, barely a century
after Captain Cook's voyages, he found
whole cultures that had surrendered
to despair: living men and women
surrounded by ghosts, and about
to become ghosts themselves.
But that is all long ago. Enough time
has elapsed for the old sorrows to have
disappeared into the past as the old
customs did before them. Such is the
way of the world, even in an earthly
heaven that was turned, for a while,
into hell. In the truncated days of the
icy French winter, what has stayed
with me—or, more accurately,
what I cling to—**are the images
of first encounters with
the islands, when Europeans,
oblivious to the seeds
of destruction they'd brought
with them, exulted in the sheer
beauty of what they'd just
discovered.**

14

1 *Paul Gauguin,* Te aa no areois
[The bread tree seed], 1892
Oil on burlap, 92.1 × 72.1 cm
New York, Museum of Modern Art

2 *Marlon Brando, another*
Westerner fascinated by the
paradisiac South Seas Islands
in the movie The Mutiny on
the Bounty *by Lewis Milestone,*
USA, 1962

3 *The legendary beauty
of Tahitian women prisoned
by the "Mother Hubbard" gown,
c. 1889*

4 *A Hawaiian quilt work,
late XIX century, made
of plain woven cotton, wool
batting, hand and machine
piecing, hand appliqué
and contour quilting*

On James Cook's first voyage
of exploration through the South Seas
in 1769, the naturalist Joseph Banks
found on Tahiti a people "so free from
deceit that I trusted myself among them
almost as freely as I could do in my own
country." What Banks would not let
himself say, of course, was that he trusted
them rather more than the people
of his own country. The original reason
for Cook's expedition to the recently
discovered island of Tahiti was to observe
from that angle deep in the Southern
Hemisphere the transit of the planet
Venus across the face of the sun and
thereby contribute to a better estimate
of the distances between the planets
of the known solar system. But after six
weeks on the islands, when the great
astronomical event happened, Banks
devoted fewer than a hundred words
to it in his log. Far more intriguing to
him was a breakfast with the island's king

and the king's sister, and a visit later
in the day from "three handsome women."
(So awkwardly repressed were the sexual
mores of the time, even among
the supposedly libertine French, that
a woman masquerading as the male valet
to the naturalist Philibert Commerçon
on the round-the-world expedition of
Count Bougainville in the 1760s managed
to disguise her gender more or less
successfully until they reached Tahiti.
At that point the largely naked locals on
the beach saw through the billowy clothes
disguising the body of 26-year-old Jeanne
"Jean" Barré in a matter of minutes.
The French, masters of self-delusion
that they were, wrote much about the
"noble savage," when the most striking
attribute of the Polynesians was common
sense unfettered, at the time, by Western
prejudice.)
Even as the Polynesian people suffered
the afflictions of civilization, the land

remained: savage, spectacular, and otherworldly. And so I believe—I imagine —it does to this day. Some seventy years after Cook's voyages, the young American Herman Melville jumped ship on the largest island in the Marquesas only to discover a landscape where reigned "the most hushed repose, which I almost feared to break, lest, like the enchanted gardens in the fairy tale, a single syllable might dissolve the spell." **Here were spectacular flowers like the delicate *tiare*, used to make the scented oil known as *monoï*. Here was food and drink for the picking on the breadfruit trees and the coconut palms. Not since Adam and Eve were cast out of Eden had such a place been seen.** Almost fifty years after Melville, Stevenson wrote about standing in the shallow water of a cove in the Marquesas beneath cliffs

draped in lianas: "The beach was lined
with palms and a tree called the purao,
something between the fig and mulberry
in growth, and bearing a flower like
a great yellow poppy with a maroon heart.
In places rocks encroached upon the
sand; the beach would be all submerged;
and the surf would bubble warmly
as high as to my knees, and play with
cocoa-nut husks as our more homely ocean
plays with wreck and wrack and bottles.
As the reflux drew down, marvels
of colour and design streamed between
my feet; which I would grasp at, miss,
or seize: now to find [among] them what
they promised, shells to grace a cabinet
or be set in gold upon a lady's finger;
now to catch only *maya* of coloured sand,
pounded fragments and pebbles,
that, as soon as they were dry,
became as dull and homely as the flints
upon a garden path. **I have toiled at
this childish pleasure for hours**

in the strong sun, conscious of my incurable ignorance; but too keenly pleased to be ashamed."

Outside my windows in Paris the snow has turned to rain, and even when the shades are drawn I hear it hammering into the courtyard like nails into ice.

I wander down the hallway of my apartment that is lined with books to search for a battered paperback left over from university days, ***Noa Noa: A Journal of the South Seas, by Paul Gauguin.***
It has traveled with me for more decades than I care to say as my books followed me from Virginia to Massachusetts to Washington DC, from there to Mexico and to Egypt and then at last to France, and I do not believe that I have read *Noa Noa* again in all that time. As I look for it I wonder if I have lost it some place.

But no, there it is among the G's,
on the same shelf as Gabriel García
Márquez. The yellowing pages fall open
as if by their own volition to the passage
where the painter, frustrated by the
embarrassingly European character that
the Tahitian capital has acquired
by the time he arrives there in 1891,
decides to trek deep into the interior.

"The river ever more erratic—brook,
torrent, waterfall—traced a strangely
capricious course and seemed sometimes
to turn back on itself...
At the bottom of the water, crayfish
of an extraordinary size looked
up at me, seeming to say, 'What are you
doing here?' and ancient eels fled
at my approach.
Suddenly, at a sharp bend I saw, leaning
against an outcropping of rock,
not so much bracing herself against
it as caressing it with both hands,

a young girl, naked. She was drinking from
a spring that gushed silently from very
high among the stones. When she had
finished drinking, letting go of the rock,
she caught the water in her hands and let
it run down between her breasts.
Then — even though I hadn't made the
slightest sound — like a fearful antelope
that senses and discovers what is foreign,
she lowered her head, peering into the
thicket where I remained motionless.
My look did not meet hers. As soon
as she saw me, she plunged into the water,
uttering the word, 'Taëhaë [ferocious].'
I rushed to look into the river: no one,
nothing — only an enormous eel that
snaked among the small stones
at the bottom."

**Was Gauguin's imagined
paradise, by the time he got
there, a matter of magical
realism, or maybe just a literary**

device, or more likely still some hallucination half-dreamed on the edge of the unconscious? Biographers and critics will tell us that of course it was some variation on fantasy. But that is fine with me. That is just what I am looking for this cold evening. I go to my computer to see what more it can give me and I type "Îles Marquises," the Marquesas Islands, onto Google Earth. The world spins until it is almost all blue. The Americas and Asia light up only the farthest thinnest edges of the globe. We are out here in the middle of nowhere in these South Seas, and now we are gliding downward through space toward minuscule points of land in the vast watery wilderness. **These are the islands where Melville jumped ship to live among the Typee, who were known as cannibals, but who cared for him, and loved**

him, until he fled them. These are the islands where Stevenson found his cove full of childish delights. **Gauguin retreated to the Marquesas to live—let's italicize that, to *live*—the last years of his life at the beginning of the twentieth century**, and the poet-singer Jacques Brel did the same in the 1970s. Brel and Gauguin are buried near each other in Calvary Cemetery above the village of Atuona on the island of Hiva Oa. The Google Earth satellite images are sharp enough to see graves, if not *their* graves. Wisps of clouds cast shadows on the richly green and rugged mountains, frozen there on the screen. **"For lack of a breeze," as Brel used to sing, "time stands still in the Marquises."** The rain outside my window has stopped. The chill has left the air in my apartment. It is late. Let the dreams begin.

François Berthoud
Born in Switzerland,
1961, lives and works in
Zurich. He is known for
his fashion illustrations.
Since the mid-1980s,
François Berthoud has
been mainly engaged
in artistic activities.
His high-impact images
bring art, fashion
and communication
together. He has
published books, staged
exhibitions and realized
special fashion projects.
He is a contributor
to major magazines
worldwide.

Christopher Dickey,
the Paris Bureau Chief
for Newsweek Magazine,
has spent much of
his life as a traveler.
Christopher's two
novels and three of his
nonfiction books grew
out of his experiences
as a war correspondent
in Central America
and the Middle East.
His widely acclaimed
memoir, Summer of
Deliverance, *tells the story*
of his relationship with
his father, the poet and
novelist James Dickey,
who first taught him
about Herman Melville
and the Marquesas, and
first showed him the
green eye of Gauguin.

The publisher would like to thank the following for the use
of their photographs in this publication, pp. 14–15:
1. Digital Image, The Metropolitan Museum of Modern Art,
New York / Scala, Florence
2. London, KPA: © 2011. Photo Scala, Florence / Heritage
Images
3. Paris, Photothèque du Musée de l'Homme
4. Queen Emma Summer Palace

cover and back cover image
by François Berthoud